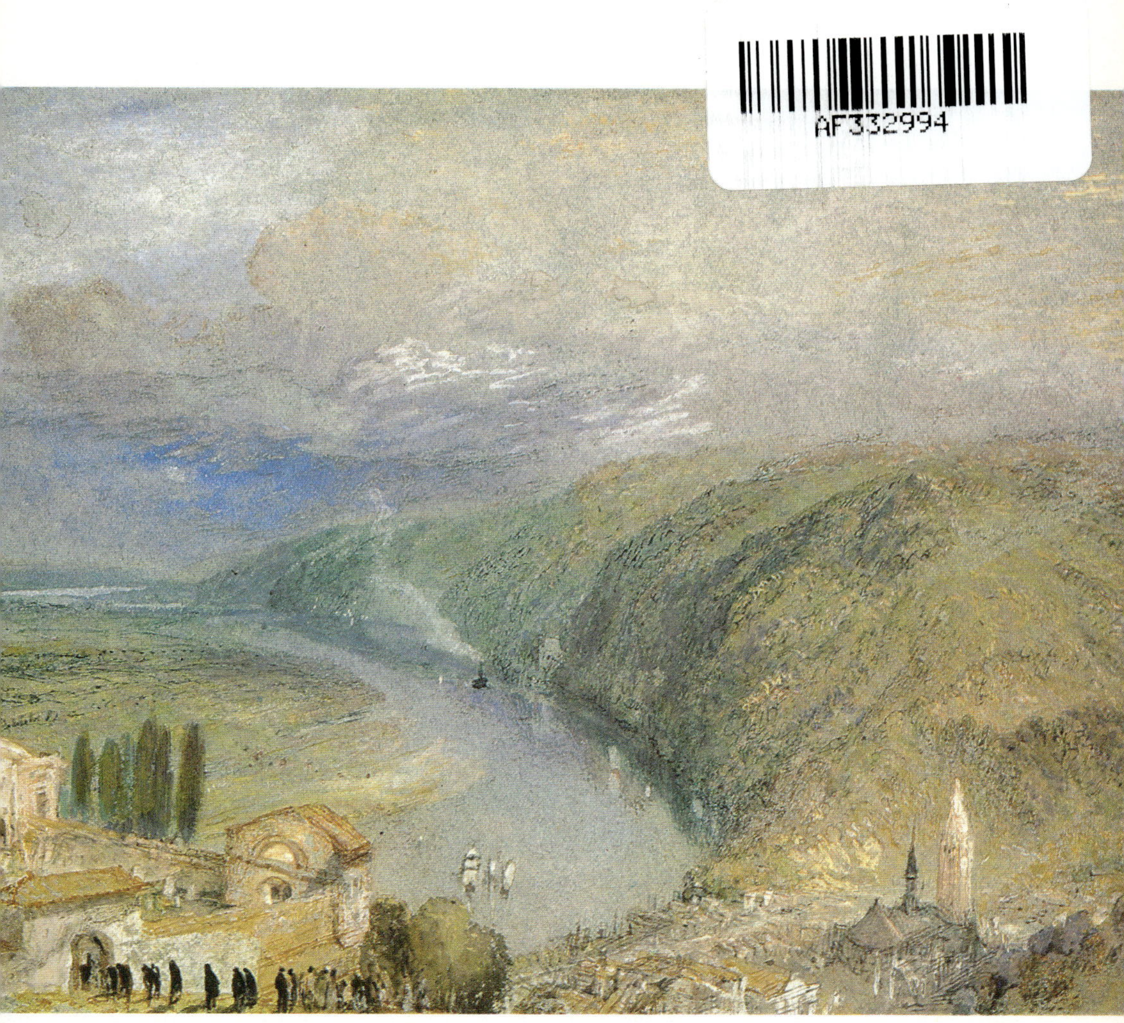

Bistre

Made from beechwood soot, and in colour indistinguishable from faded iron-gall ink, it was less frequently employed in drawing. The general terms 'pen and brown ink' or 'pen and brown wash' are now more usual.

Bodycolour

Lead white (often called Chinese white), which is mixed with pigment in order to make it opaque. Dürer used bodycolour when he made studies of landscape, flowers or animals, as did Rubens and Van Dyck, sometimes pure and sometimes in combination with watercolour (q.v.). Turner also made extensive use of bodycolour, usually with watercolour.

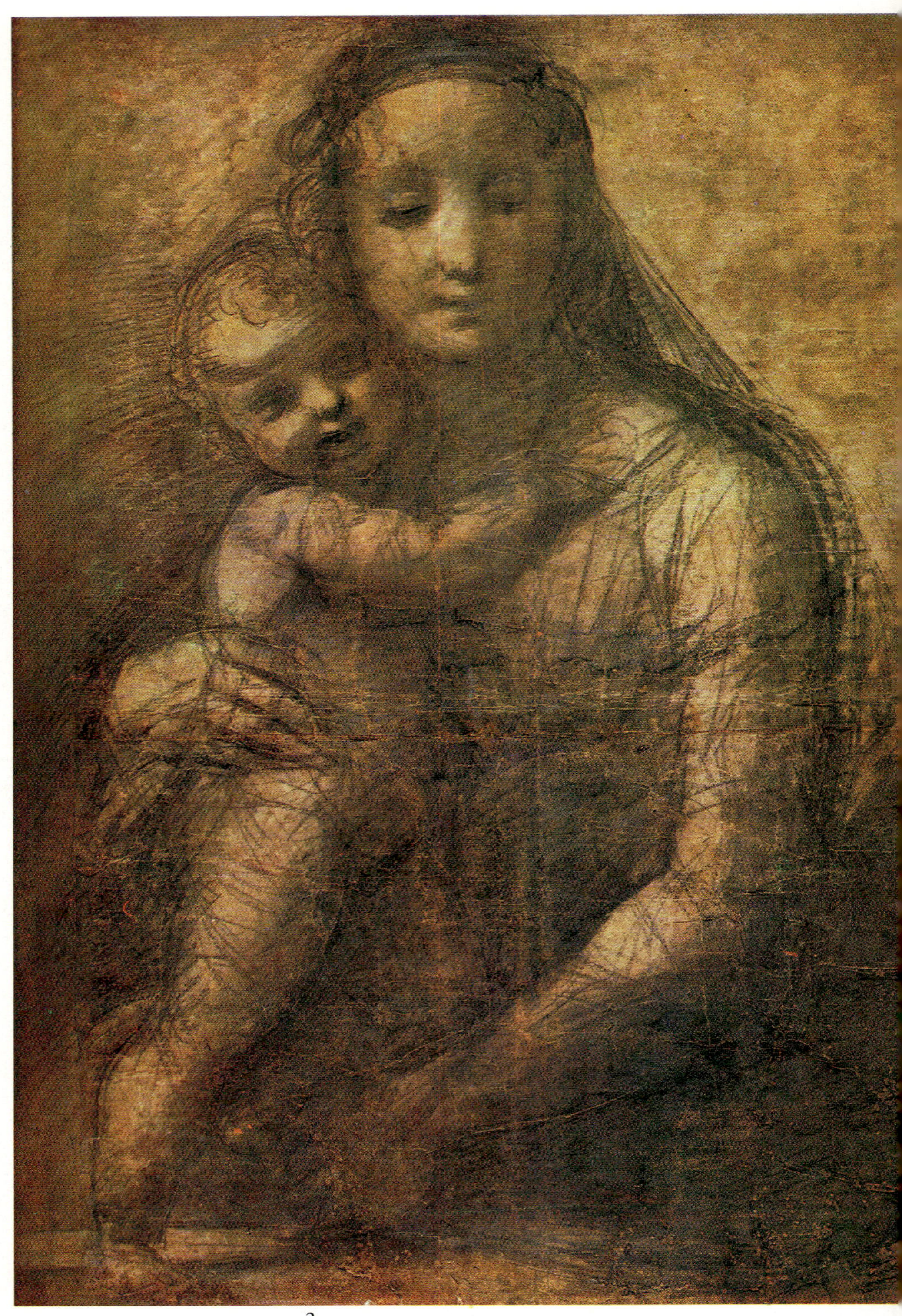

Cartoon

A full-size preparatory drawing for a painting, prepared in the studio from a small finished drawing or *modello.* The enlargement was made by means of squaring, that is by ruling the same number of horizontal and perpendicular lines in the same spacing on the small drawing and on the paper destined for the cartoon, to facilitate a proportional enlargement. In the case of a fresco the completed cartoon was applied in sections to the wall and the outlines traced through on the wet plaster. The cartoon would be ruined by being applied to the damp plaster and if it was necessary to preserve it for future use in the studio, the outline could be pricked through on to another piece of paper which could be placed on the wall. Examples of cartoons in the British Museum collection are the *Epifania* by Michelangelo, made for a pupil, Ascanio Condivi, and the *Virgin and Child* by Raphael, which corresponds with the ruined and totally repainted *Madonna of the Tower* in the National Gallery, known also as the *Mackintosh Madonna.*

An **auxiliary cartoon** is a term coined by the German art-historian Oskar Fischel to describe a full-size study based on a tracing from the complete cartoon, of details such as heads or hands which the artist wanted to realise with particular care. It was a method particularly used by Raphael.

The word 'cartoon' has also a modern meaning remote from its original definition. It is held to be a humorous or sarcastic comment on a current topic, frequently political, and often depicting in allegorical terms a known situation. This modern usage dates from 1843 when an exhibition was held in Westminster Hall of cartoons from which a design was to be selected for the fresco decoration of the new Houses of Parliament. *Punch* humorously professed to run alongside the great competing artists and John Leech's drawing in no. 105 of the magazine was the first caricature to be called a cartoon. It was entitled 'Substance and Shadow: the Poor ask for Bread, and the Philanthropy of the State accords an Exhibition'.

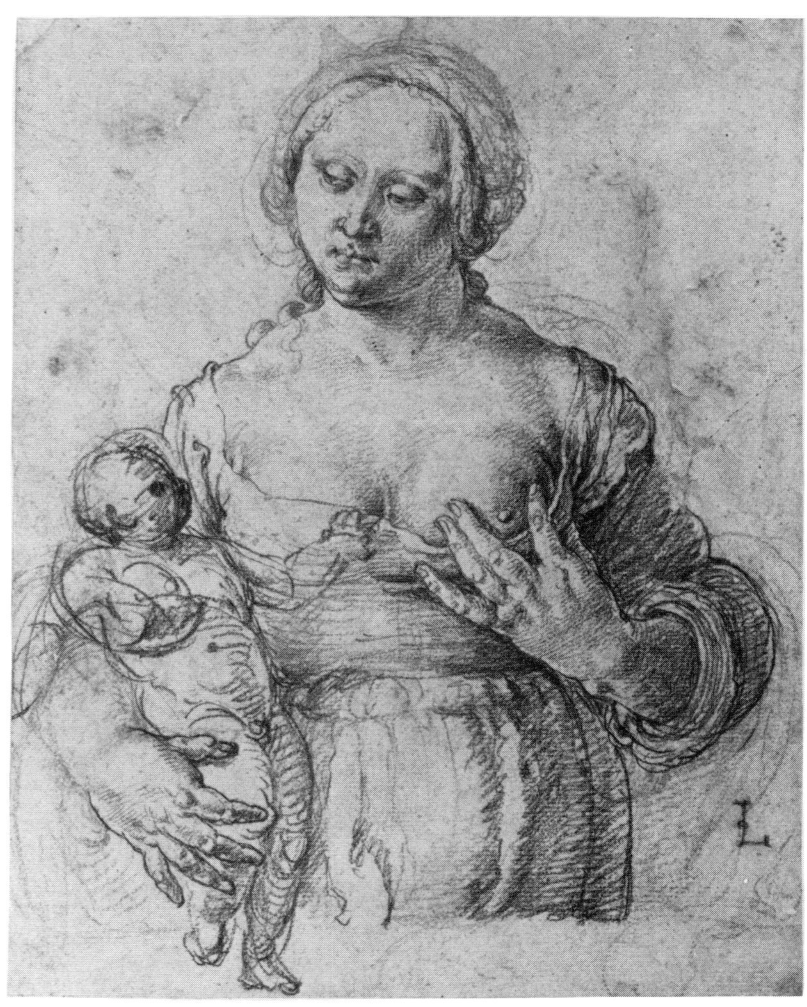

1. **Black Chalk** (sometimes called Italian chalk) is a mineral which is very adhesive to paper and indelible. Small pieces were shaved down to a point and used in a metal holder. What is called black chalk today is a composite substance darker than Italian chalk.

2. **Red Chalk** was used in drawing a little before 1500 and its first great master was Leonardo da Vinci (1452–1519). Rubbing with the finger, brush or **stump** (q.v.) brought about subtle gradations of tone. Correggio (1489/94–1534) was a great master of this technique which he achieved by the addition of white chalk which produced reflected light in the shadows.

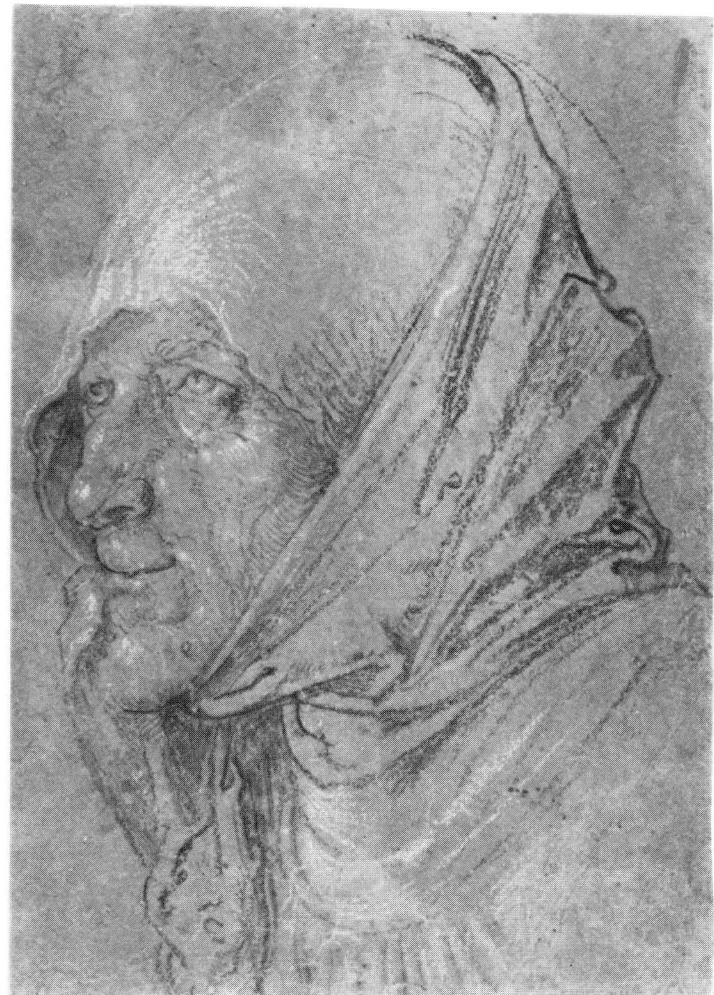

Black chalk (left):
Lucas van Leyden
(1494–1533)
Study for a Virgin
and Child.
Black chalk.
210 × 171 mm.
1892 – 8 – 4 – 15.

Charcoal (right):
Albrecht Dürer
(1471–1528)
Head of an Old
Woman.
Charcoal, heightened
with white chalk,
on red tinted paper.
260 × 188 mm.
Sloane 5218 – 36.

Charcoal

A commonly used medium in drawing because it was cheap and easy to manufacture. Its disadvantage was that it could be easily rubbed away. No means of fixing charcoal seems to have been discovered before the first quarter of the sixteenth century. However, it must have been well known at this period because charcoal together with white chalk on blue paper was a favourite medium of Venetian painters such as Titian and Tintoretto. Charcoal sticks were sometimes dipped in linseed oil and this made the line indelible but the oil left behind a yellow streak on either side. Guercino (1591–1666) was one artist who drew with this particular kind of charcoal.

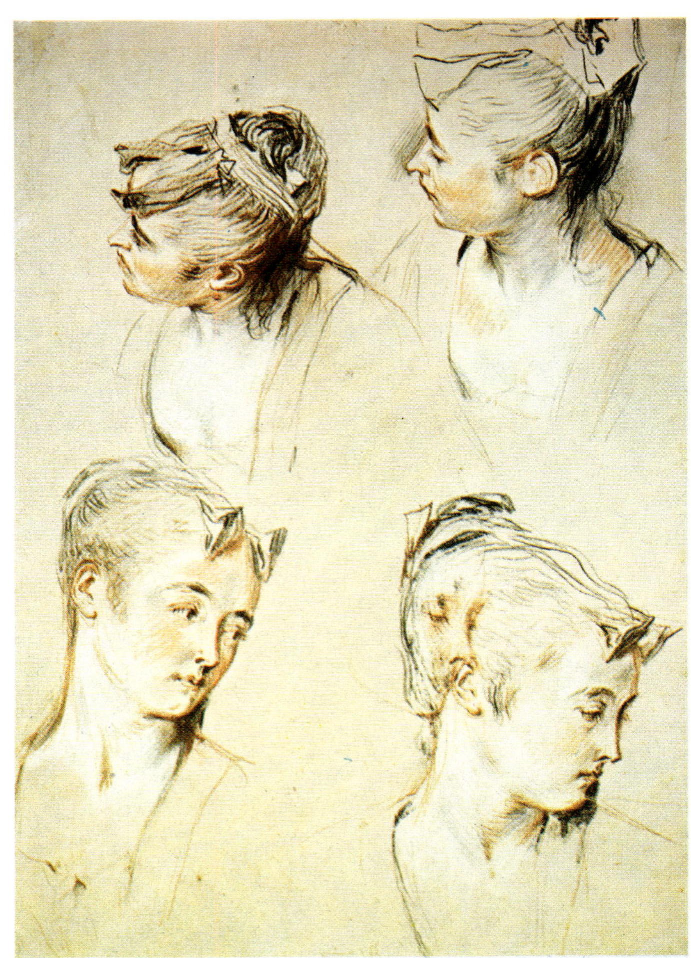

Crayon

See **pastel**. Modern 'crayons', made of synthetic substances are more oily than the crayon used most extensively in eighteenth-century France when the term meant the use of different coloured chalks.

Aux trois crayons

The combination of red, black and white chalks on a yellowish or off-white paper was used particularly successfully by Watteau (1684–1721).

Conté (crayon)

In 1790, Nicolas Jacques Conté (1755–1805), a French chemist, invented the 'Conté' Crayon which was a mixture of refined graphite and clay. It was intended as a substitute for the **lead pencil** (q.v.), when during the Napoleonic Wars, simple plumbago was in short supply.

Collector's mark

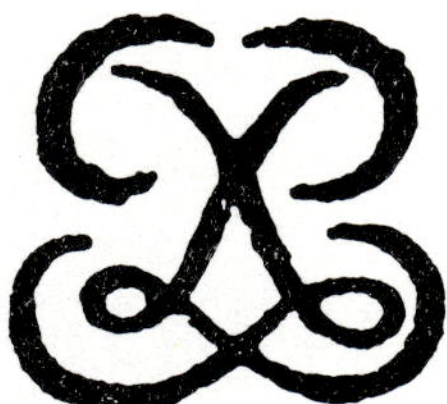

The collector's mark of
Sir Peter Lely (1618–1680)

A small distinctive mark, usually composed of initials, sometimes hand written but more often stamped, which is applied by collectors to indicate their ownership or posthumously to indicate that a drawing has formed part of a particular collection. The earliest mark known is that of Sir Peter Lely (1618–80). His mark was put on his drawings by his executors after his death. The standard work on collectors' marks is *Les Marques de Collections de Dessins et D'Estampes* by Frits Lugt, Amsterdam, 1921 (Supplement 1956). A 'Studio Stamp' was applied to drawings found in the artist's studio, sometime after his death. Such stamps are a useful but not infallible guide to authenticity.

Écorché

(French – 'skinned') An anatomical subject with the skin removed so as to display the muscles for study; the term also refers to drawings of such subjects.

(fl)

'Flourished'. A term used when the exact dates of an artist's birth and death are not known, to indicate the approximate period of his activity.

Écorché : Parmigianino (1503–40). An *écorché* right arm. Pen and brown wash over red chalk. 128 × 77 mm. 1905 – 11 – 10 – 15.

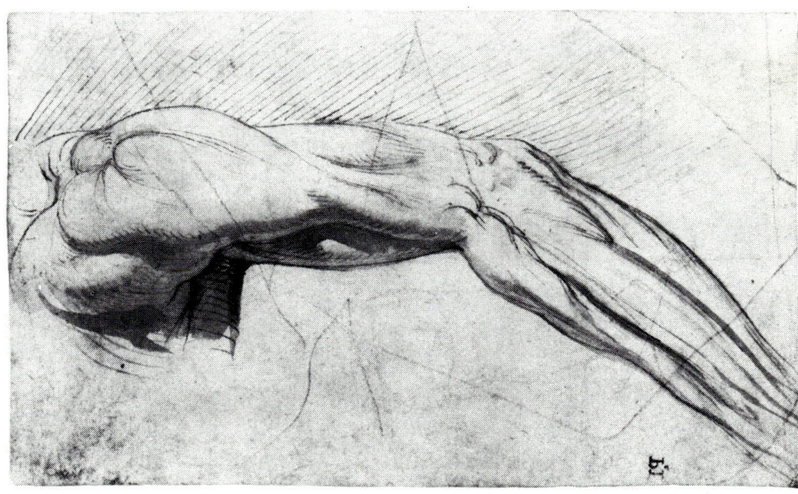

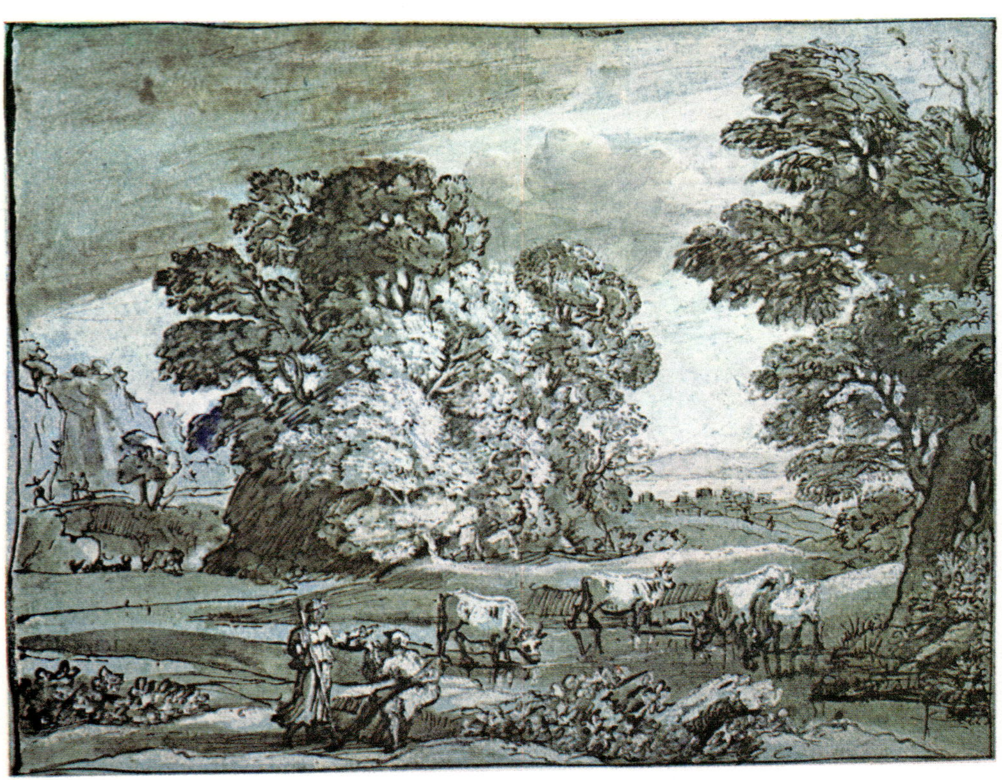

Gouache	Either a drawing executed entirely in bodycolour or a watercolour pigment made opaque by the addition of gum or honey.
Heighten	Highlights are obtained either by the addition of a lighter bodycolour or chalk, or by scraping down to the white paper.
Ink	Iron-gall writing ink, prepared from an iron-salt and tannin, was also the chief drawing medium from the fifteenth until the eighteenth century. Indian or Chinese ink consists essentially of lamp-black mixed with gum and hardened by baking. Its colour does not fade but it reacts to moisture. It was rarely used in Italy in the fifteenth and sixteenth centuries, but was common in Germany during the same period, its use being almost as frequent as that of iron-gall ink.

The colour of iron-gall ink, originally almost black, changes with age to various tones of brown and yellow. The characteristic brown colour of so many 'Old Master' drawings is probably not original but brought about by chemical change.

Inscribed

An artist's name is said to be 'inscribed' and not 'signed' if it was written by someone else.

Inscriptions

Titles or descriptions or attributions written on a drawing, not always by the artist himself.

Inventory numbers

The series of numbers on the mounts (e.g. 1974 – 12 – 9 – 4) shows when the particular print or drawing entered the collection and also identifies the work. The date above means that the item was the fourth acquired on the ninth of December 1974.

Old collections bear inventory numbers in a different arrangement. A drawing which entered the Museum before 1808 (when the Print Room was set up as a department separate from the Library) is marked by the number (of four figures) of the album which contained it, followed by a second number giving the order of its arrangement in the album, e.g., 5217–20. In 1837 a general inventory of the collection was made and each print or drawing was given a letter or two letters, (A–Z and Aa–Pp), followed by two groups of numbers, e.g., 0.5–20; Ee. 3–127.

Heightening (opposite):
Claude Lorrain
(1600–82)
Pastoral landscape (1650)
Pen, brown wash;
extensive white heightening.
197 × 261 mm.
Liber Veritatis No. 121.

Inscriptions:
Claude Lorrain (1600–82)
An elderly shepherd, seated.
Pen and brown ink.
194 × 266 mm.
Liber Veritatis No. 4 *verso.*
Inscribed lower right, *faict pour/paris* and below it on another occasion, *Claudio fecit/in V.R.*
Numbered 4, at top left, top right (18th century) and bottom centre beside Claude's monogram.

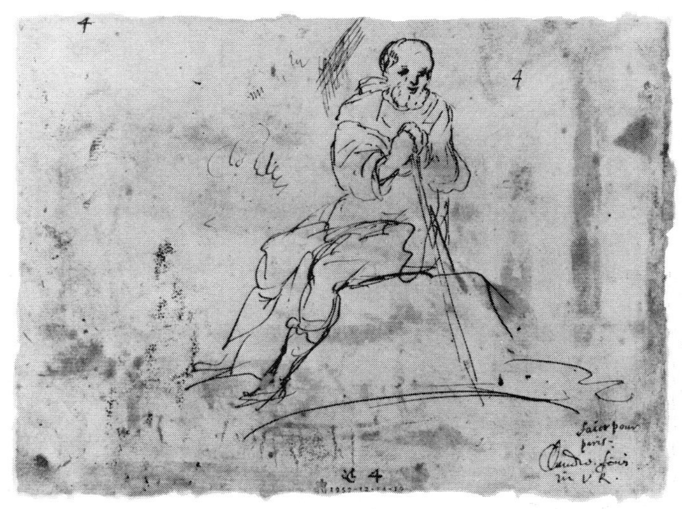

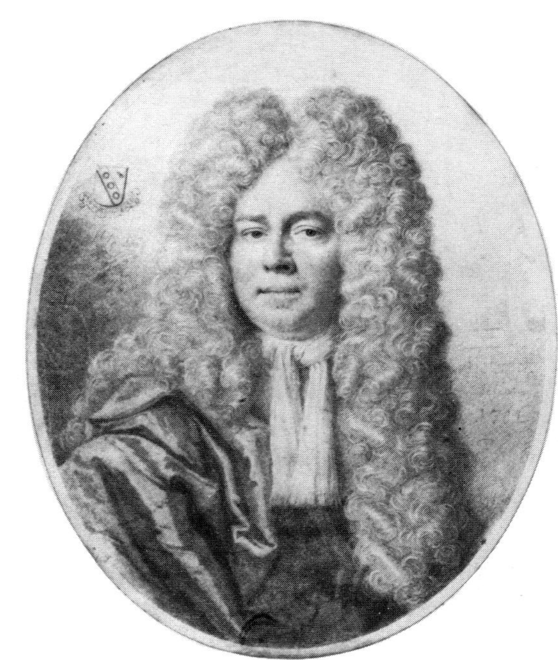

Lead pencil

'Plumbago' and 'black lead' are terms used to denote a crystalline form of carbon, more strictly called graphite and now generally included in the description 'pencil'. This was first used in the sixteenth century but it did not become as widely employed as it is today before the eighteenth century. Lead pencil leaves a shiny deposit on the paper while black chalk (with which it is sometimes confused) leaves a duller deposit as well as being more consistently grey in tone.

Lead point

An instrument with a point of lead, or an alloy of lead and tin, was used in the fifteenth and sixteenth centuries in preparation for a drawing in pen and ink, black chalk, or some other medium. The lead point was hard and indented the surface of the paper, but the mark it made was very faint. Occasionally, lead-point was used for the whole drawing. It was a conveniently portable implement before the invention of the lead pencil.

Metalpoint

An instrument with a point of gold or silver was used in combination with a prepared paper. This technique was in frequent use in the fifteenth and earlier sixteenth centuries

10

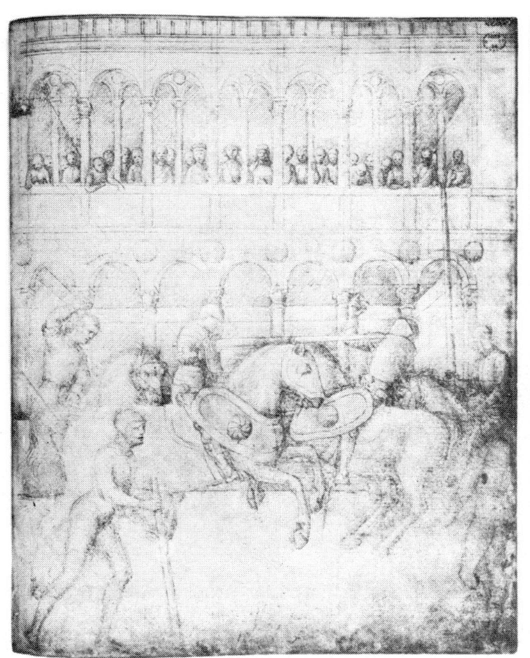 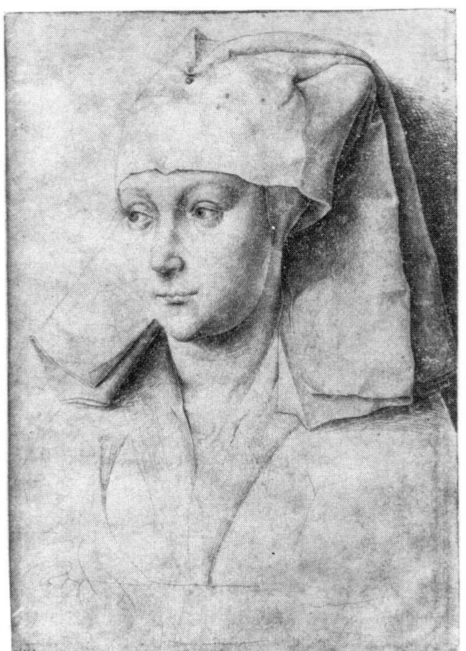

in Italy, the Netherlands and Germany. The ground was composed of powdered bones mixed with gum-water and applied to the paper in several coats. Its natural tone was off-white but it could be mixed with any pigment. In Italy, particularly in Florence in the fifteenth century, and in Germany many highly coloured grounds were used. The highlights were usually put in with the brush and white bodycolour. This type of coloured ground was also sometimes used for drawings in brush or pen and ink by such artists as Federico Zuccaro in the later sixteenth century.

Metalpoint was especially suitable for small sketch books for the pocket. Two sheets by Raphael: *Studies for an infant Christ* (P and G23), and *Heads of the Virgin and Child* (P and G24) from Fischel's 'Pink Sketchbook' are in the British Museum collection. (Fischel, O., *Die Zeichnungen der Umbrer*, Berlin 1917).

The technique was revived in the later nineteenth century by such artists as Alphonse Legros (1837–1911).

Measurements   Drawings are given in centimetres or millimetres with the height preceding the width.

11

Monogram (left):
The monogram of
Albrecht Dürer (1471–1528)

Pen and brown wash (right):
Rembrandt van Rijn
(1606–69)
The Good Samaritan. *c.*1642.
Pen and brown wash.
184 × 287 mm.
1860 – 6 – 16 – 122

Reed pen (lower right):
Rembrandt van Rijn
(1606–69)
Christ walking on the waves.
Reed pen and brown ink.
190 × 290 mm.
1910 – 2 – 12 – 180.

Monogram

A character composed of two or more letters interwoven, usually the initials of a name, sometimes used as a signature.

Paper

The material chiefly used for drawing by European artists. Early papers were made from rags, damped and pounded, then put on to a woven wire tray which allowed the moisture in the pulp to drain away leaving the paper; hence the term 'wove' paper.
'Laid' paper was constructed in a mould dipped into a vat of suspended wires. It has a ribbed appearance from the parallel wires in the mould. (See also **watermarks**.)

Parchment

A writing material made from the skins of animals, usually of sheep or goats. Because of its smooth surface a very fine line could be obtained. Its ivory tone and the way in which the ink dried gave a rich effect. It was chiefly used before paper was readily available although artists such as Jacopo Bellini (*c.*1400–1470/1) employed it occasionally. It was sometimes used by later artists because of the particular results obtainable. (See **vellum**.)

Pastel

Variously coloured chalks were used in pastel drawing. Although known as early as the fifteenth century, when Leonardo da Vinci wrote in the 'Codex Atlanticus' that

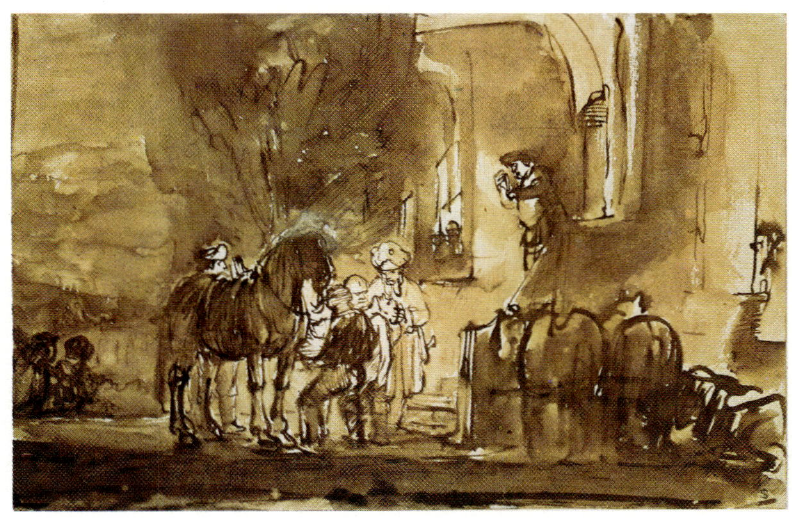

he learned this technique from a Frenchman, it was not until the eighteenth century in France that pastel drawings became popular. However, Federico Barocci (1535–1612) made many studies in a technique of coloured chalks peculiar to him.

Pen and wash

Feathers were generally used for pens. The reed pen often employed by Rembrandt was capable of great variations of width of line according to the way the pen was held.

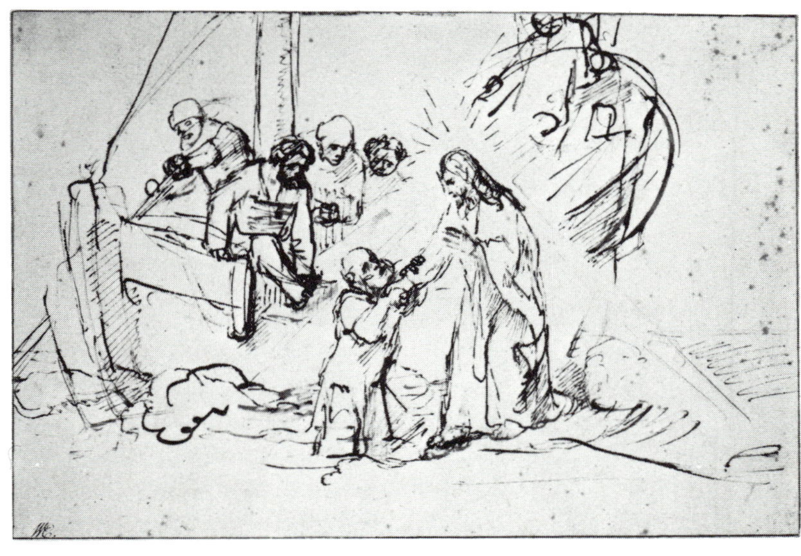

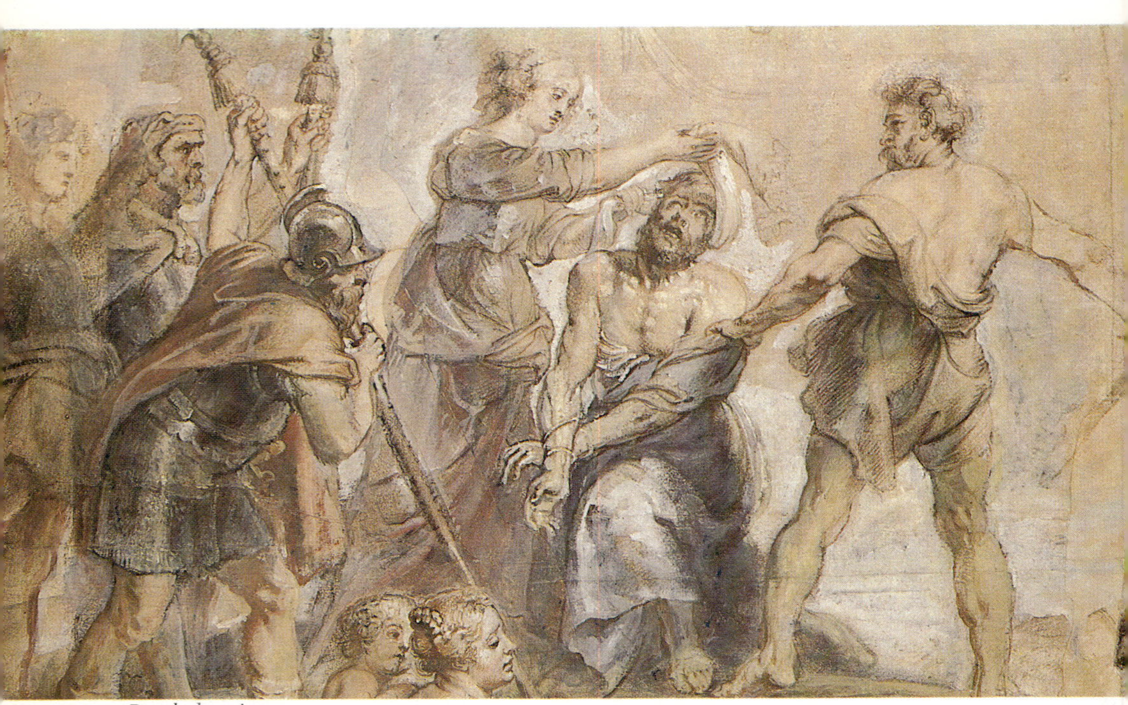

Brush drawing:
Peter Paul Rubens
(1577–1640)
Detail of the
Martyrdom of St Paul.
Brush drawing in oil colours,
over an underdrawing in
black chalk.
710 × 515 mm.
N.G. 853–E. 1973 U.1357.

'Wash' denotes a sweep or area of tone applied with the brush. A drawing is sometimes said to be in 'pen and ink', but on closer examination with a magnifying glass, the line is frequently seen to be drawn with a fine brush. The example shown, by Rubens, is pure brush drawing over an underdrawing in black chalk.

Pentimento

(Italian: repentance) An indication in a drawing or painting of the artist's change of mind.

Recto

The more important side of a sheet drawn on both sides. Also the right-hand page of an opening in a bound volume, irrespective of which if any side is drawn on.

Scraping out

The removal of paint with a knife, sharp instrument or the point of the brush or even the finger nail, to expose the paper beneath and produce a highlight of white. The term is nearly always applied to watercolours and Turner often used this technique. (See also **heighten**.)

14

Sepia

A rich dark brown colour obtained from the inky secretion of the cuttle fish. It does not seem to have been known before the eighteenth century or to have been generally used until the nineteenth. The term is often used as a synonym for dark brown.

Stump

A coil of leather or paper ending in a point, which was used for rubbing on chalk and pastel drawings.

Vellum

The highest quality parchment made from the selected skin of young animals (originally calves). (See **parchment**.)

Verso

The opposite of **recto** (q.v.).

Vignette

A small ornamental engraving or design used usually in book-illustration, the essential feature being that it has no finite shape, the edges shading off into the surrounding paper.

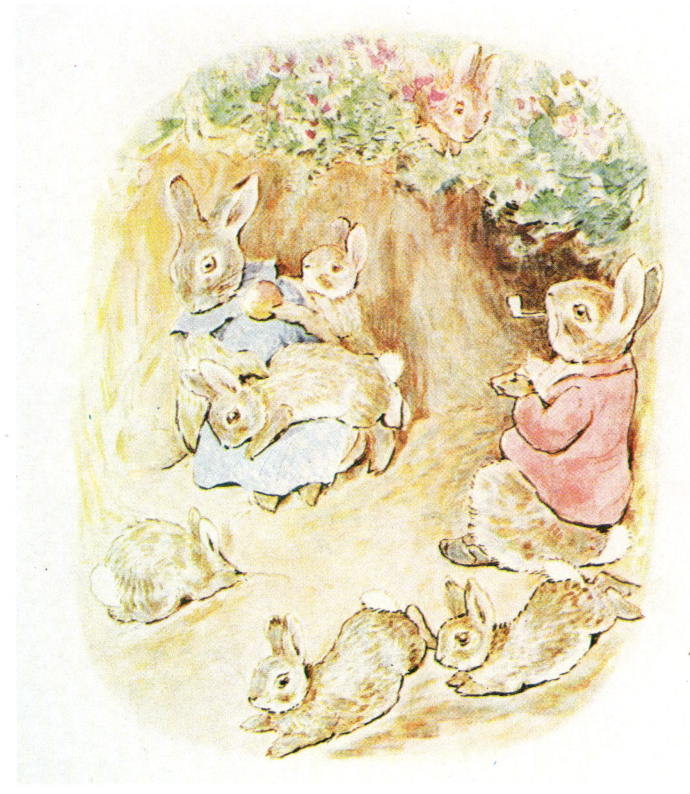

Vignette:
Beatrix Potter
(1866–1943)
Illustration on page 11
of *The Tale of The Flopsy Bunnies*
(1909).
in pen and
ink, pencil;
watercolour.
111 × 94 mm.
1946 – 11 – 21 – 4.

Watercolour

Colours mixed with gum and soluble in water. The brilliancy of 'pure' watercolour (see **bodycolour**) occurs because it is transparent so that the white surface of the paper remains as the lighting agent. Most watercolour papers have a granulous surface and the little hollows and projections provide an alternation of light and half light.

Watermarks

Devices or trade marks used by paper-manufacturers. Particulars as to date and area of origin of the paper can be deduced from the watermark but rarely, even when it actually contains a date, can a watermark provide more than a *terminus post quem*. A major work on early water-marks is C. M. Briquet, *'Les Filigranes: Dictionnaire historique des marques du papier dès leur apparition vers 1282'*, 4 vols., Paris 1907. For later ones see W. A. Churchill, *Watermarks in Paper*, Amsterdam 1935.

Watermark:
A watermark used by the English firm of James Whatman, working 1760–1850.
Coat-of-Arms. Date 1777.

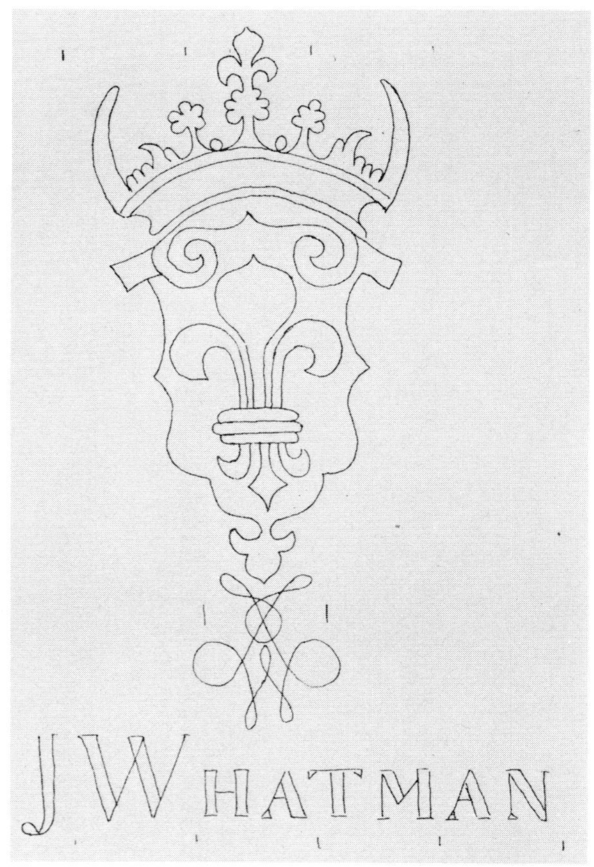